T0381458

Proceed with
Confidence

Proceed with Confidence

Insight through Reflection
and Experience

Diane La Pierre

Artist
Alexa Cifelli

Rev. date: 12/30/2024

To order additional copies of this book, contact:
Xlibris
844-714-8691
www.Xlibris.com
Orders@Xlibris.com
860664

For my children and grandchildren

May you always know

Peace

Happiness

Laughter

Joy

Love

When a dilemma arises

And no one is near

Open to a page

And listen to what you hear

You know right from wrong,

and wrong is *never* an option.

There are two paths,

the right one and the wrong one.

Always choose right.

You become the happiest

when **helping** others.

Hate cannot drive out hate;

only *love* can do that.

Martin Luther King, Jr.

Listen to your conscience.

It will *never* lie to you!

Be true to yourself.

Like attracts like.

You are a culmination of everyone and

everything that you have seen and heard.

Choose wisely.

Just be who you are

because you are great!

Common sense always

paves the way.

Learn from the mistakes of others.

You are smart.

Trust your inner thoughts.

Use your imagination

to **create** wonders.

Positive thinking creates

positive thoughts.

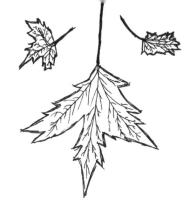

Sometimes *great* ideas

happen when you are sleeping.

Confidence is gained

through your experiences.

The only person you

can make happy

is yourself.

Knowledge gives you the

self-confidence

to succeed.

Stand up for truth, and you will

be respected.

Never fear being alone

because it strengthens

your character.

Do what **inspires** you!

Happiness comes from within.

Ask questions.

No one knows everything.

Force positive thoughts!

Choose peace.

Mistakes become the *best* teacher.

The only person you can change is

yourself.

$\mathcal{D}$ig deep.

The answer lies **within** you.

Dreams don't work unless *you* do.

Reach for the stars,

then reach higher.

YOU are worth it!!!

Always be a *good* friend.

You don't always have to be right.

It is **okay** if you make mistakes.

You are a strong person

who can do

amazing things!

You are **perfectly**

imperfect.

Always be thankful!

You have to respect yourself

before you can gain the respect of others.

You learn more from listening.

$\mathcal{B}$e a **good** sport.

W here you are

is *exactly* where you need to be.

Be **proud** of who you are,

and where you came from.

Be helpful to others.

L earn from **your** mistakes

and from the mistakes of others.

B_e understanding.

You are not perfect.

No one is.

Be grateful for what you have.

Always keep your promise.

The grass is **never** greener

on the other side.

Wherever you go,

go with *all* your heart.

Confucius

In the waves of change,

we find our direction.

The difference between winning and losing

is

most

often

not

quitting.

Walt Disney

Learn each day.

Love each moment.

Lend a hand where you can.

The greatest glory in living lies

not in never failing, but in

rising every time we fail.

Nelson Mandela

Positive thoughts

lead to positive outcomes.

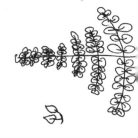

Life is what happens while you are making

other plans.

John Lennon

The future belongs to those who believe

in the beauty of their dreams.

Eleanor Roosevelt

Well *done* is better than well said.

Benjamin Franklin

$\mathcal{D}$o not go where the path may lead,

go instead where there is no path and

leave

a

trail.

Ralph Waldo Emerson

$\mathcal{B}$e kind,

for **everyone** you meet

is fighting a hard battle.

Plato

Be the *change* you wish to see in the world.

Mahatma Gandhi

Don't cry because it's over.

Smile because it happened.

Dr. Seuss

You're braver than you believe,
stronger than you seem, and
smarter than you think.

Christopher Robin/A.A.Milne

Discipline is the bridge between

goals and accomplishments.

$\mathcal{I}$f you are going to do something,

do it right!

B_ehumble.

When times are tough or too hard to bear,

remember you are stronger than you think

and with that

you will always prevail.

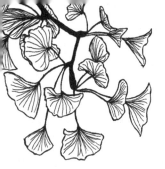

$\mathcal{D}$on't let fear hold you back

from being the person

you

know

you

are!

Be yourself.

Everyone else is already taken.

Oscar Wilde

The mind is everything.

What you **think**

you

become.

Buddha

Your time is limited.

Don't waste it

living someone else's life.

Steve Jobs

The measure of intelligence is the ability

to *change.*

Albert Einstein

*S*uccess is not final.

Failure is not fatal.

It is the *courage* to continue that

counts.

Winston Churchill

If you want to lift yourself up,

lift up *someone* else.

Booker T. Washington

The journey of a thousand miles

begins with a

single

step.

Lao Tzu

It does not matter how slowly you go,

as long as you *do not* stop.

Confucius

I t takes courage to grow up and

become who you really are.

E. E. Cummings

The only person you are

destined to become

is the person you *decide* to be.

Ralph Waldo Emerson

You miss 100% of the shots you *don't* take.

Wayne Gretzky

*S*uccess is falling nine times

and getting *UP* ten.

Jon Bon Jovi

A person who never made a mistake

never tried anything new.

Albert Einstein

Happiness is not something ready-made.

It comes from your **OWN** actions.

Dalai Lama

Everything you have ever wanted is

sitting on the other side of fear.

George Addair

You'll never get bored

when you try something new.

There's really no limit

to what you can *do.*

Dr. Seuss

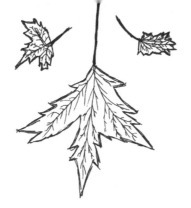

There is no **substitute** for hard work!

Thomas Edison

Never let the fear of striking out

keep you from playing the game.

Babe Ruth

No act of kindness, no matter how small,

is

ever

wasted.

Aesop

I find that the *harder* I work,

the more *luck* I seem to have.

Thomas Jefferson

The time is always right

to *do* what is right.

Martin Luther King, Jr.

Life isn't about finding yourself.

Life is about *creating* yourself.

George Bernard Shaw

Before anything else,

preparation is the key to success.

Alexander Graham Bell

A little progress adds up to

big results.

I am who I am today

because of the choices I made

yesterday!

Eleanor Roosevelt

*C*hange can be *good*!

Remember caterpillars become

butterflies.

Nobody can make you feel inferior

without *your* consent.

Eleanor Roosevelt

Go **confidently** in the direction of your

dreams!

Live

the

life

you've

imagined.

Henry David Thoreau

Life is made of

happy

moments!

You gain knowledge through your

experiences.

*C*lap for others.

Your time **will** come!

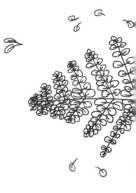

I t is okay to say . . .

I'm sorry.

I was wrong.

I made a mistake.

Always follow the rules!

Choose options that inspire!

Be the **best** version of yourself!

Smile today!

Printed in the United States
by Baker & Taylor Publisher Services